Buildings for the Age

new building types 1900-1939

Alastair Forsyth

GENERAL EDITOR
Peter Fowler

ROYAL COMMISSION ON HISTORICAL MONUMENTS ENGLAND

LONDON HER MAJESTY'S STATIONERY OFFICE

ISBN 0 11 700998 9

HER MAJESTY'S STATIONERY OFFICE

Government Bookshops

49 High Holborn, London WC1V 6HB
13a Castle Street, Edinburgh EH2 3AR
41 The Hayes, Cardiff CF1 1JW
Brazennose Street, Manchester M60 8AS
Southey House, Wine Street, Bristol BS1 2BQ
258 Broad Street, Birmingham B1 2HE
80 Chichester Street, Belfast BT1 4JY

Government publications are also available
through booksellers

ACKNOWLEDGEMENTS

The Commission is grateful for permission to reproduce photographs in the National Monuments Record of which the copyright is held by:
Architectural Press
B.W.S. Publishing (*Architect and Building News*)
Elmbridge Borough Council

The author thanks Mr R. Almond (Shoreham Airport), Mr Ball (Deputy Planning Officer, Elmbridge Borough Council), Mrs M. Barton (Asst. Curator, Weybridge Museum), Mr G. Fleming (Hon. Secretary, Brooklands Society), Mr Hancocks (British Aerospace), Mr Hatt (Bedfordshire County Council), Mr A. Jeffcoate (British Aerospace), Mrs A. Lansdell (Curator, Weybridge Museum), London Film Productions, Mr C. Manton (Museum of London), Mr Milton (Manager, Shoreham Airport), Mr G. M. Warren (HMSO). The author also thanks numerous colleagues on the Commission staff, especially Miss J. Carden, Mr R. Flanders, Mrs D. Kendall and staff in the Order Section, Mr J. D. M. Leith, and Mr R. Parsons and staff in the Photographic Section.

(*front cover*) City Airport, Speke, Merseyside. Architect: R. Arthur Landstein, 1937. N.M.R. 1981. (*inside front cover*) Palace Cinema, Kentish Town, London. Bedford Lemere, 1913. (*inside back cover*) New Victoria Cinema, Westminster, London. Architect: E. Wamsley-Lewis, 1930. Herbert Felton, October 1930. Copyright: *Architect and Building News* (B. W. S. Publishing).

Printed in England for Her Majesty's Stationery Office
by Balding + Mansell, Wisbech
Dd. 0699046 C80

EDITOR'S FOREWORD

All the photographs in this book are held in the National Monuments Record (NMR), a national archive which is part of the Royal Commission on Historical Monuments (England). The NMR originated in 1941 as the National Buildings Record which, at a time when so much was being destroyed, took upon itself the task of photographing as many historic buildings as possible before it was too late. The Record continued its work after the War and was transferred to the Royal Commission in 1963. As the NMR it now covers both architectural and archaeological subjects and has over a million photographs, together with maps, plans and other documents, relating to England's man-made heritage. The NMR is a public archive, open from 10.00 – 17.30 hours on weekdays; prints can be supplied to order on payment of the appropriate fee.

This book is the second of a series intended to illustrate the wealth of photographic material publicly available in the NMR. Many of the photographs are valuable in their own right, either because of their age or because of the photographer who took them or because they are the only records we now possess of buildings, and even whole environments, which have disappeared. Unlike other Commission publications, these are primarily picture-books, drawing entirely on what happens to be in the NMR. There is no attempt to treat each subject comprehensively nor to accompany it with a deeply researched text, but the text and captions are intended to give meaning to the photographs by indicating the context within which they can be viewed. It would be pleasing if they suggested lines of enquiry to others to follow up.

The early titles in the series will show where the strengths of the archive lie. Equally, of course, the collection is weak in some respects and I hope that many of those who buy this volume may be reminded of old, and perhaps disregarded, photographs of buildings in their possession. We would be glad to be told of the whereabouts of such photographs as potential contributions to a national record of our architectural heritage.

Despite the modest ambitions of this book, that it comes from a body concerned with *historical* monuments is perhaps worth brief comment. This is in fact the first Commission publication concerned at any level exclusively with twentieth-century material. It reflects the situation that, although the Commission's original fieldwork, investigation and record traditionally stop *c* 1850, the NMR is open-ended in its collecting activities: history, and its monuments too, stop (or start) yesterday.

Royal Commission on Historical
Monuments (England)
Fortress House,
23 Savile Row,
London W1X 1AB

Peter Fowler,
Secretary,
Royal Commission on
Historical Monuments (England);
General Editor,
NMR Photographic Archives

FURTHER READING

Architectural Design Vol. 49 No. 10–11, *Britain in the Thirties*. 1979.
David Atwell, *Cathedrals of Entertainment*. Architectural Press 1980.
Charles Gardner, *Fifty Years of Brooklands*. Heinemann 1956.
Ed. Jennifer Hawkins and Marianne Hollis, *Thirties*. Arts Council 1979.
A. McCall, *Green Line. A History of London's Country Bus Services*. A.B.P. 1980.
J. Morton Shand, *Modern Cinemas*. Architectural Press 1936.
Dennis Sharp, *The Picture Palace*. Evelyn 1969.
Leonard Stevens, *Byfleet, A Village in England*. n.d.

Buildings for the Age

INTRODUCTION

The first three decades of the twentieth century witnessed considerable changes and developments in English architecture. New possibilities arose as a result of technological developments, while social changes created new demands. Some buildings, especially of new types for new functions, were particularly appropriate to the age in which they were built; a number have remained highly relevant in the succeeding years. Above all, the first three decades of the twentieth century produced innovatory buildings. Invariably the novelty of the buildings was reflected in their appearance, but in the main it was their purpose that was new. Such buildings have now come to be taken rather for granted, but it should be remembered that most of them were the source of considerable comment when they were planned or built. No claim is made to present here anything like a full survey but it is hoped that this selection gives an impression of the range of these exciting structures and will encourage the reader to look again at what might at first seem humdrum or even *passé*. It is particularly relevant at a time when the historical significance of many twentieth-century buildings is only beginning to be assessed and when

several of interest have already been demolished.

One of the most significant developments to affect our modern lives and our buildings has been, obviously, the advent of the motor car. Invented at the end of the nineteenth century, the motor car began to appear in numbers in the first decade of the present century. Most early models were manufactured in Europe, but moves were made to stimulate a British motor industry in 1906/7 when Hugh Fortescue Locke King, the famous civil engineer, built a huge private motor circuit at Brooklands, his estate in Surrey. There, motor engineers were encouraged to develop their designs and demonstrate their results to the public at racing spectacles. A unique feature of the track's design was the saucer rim, which eliminated corners and thus enabled cars to race at continuous speed.

Meanwhile, far from the roar of engines and clouds of dust, motor cars were on display in the showrooms of the West End. In the period before the First World War, ownership of what was an article of luxury was more or less restricted to the noble or the very wealthy. Thus Bond Street in Mayfair was an appropriate venue for Darracq's showroom, proving that the motor car had become socially desirable. The needs of the motor car in turn spawned such buildings as Michelin's and Mitchell's Motors with its useful and forward-looking lift. After the First World War, there was a considerable increase in the number of privately owned cars, particularly as models were increasingly mass-produced. By the end of the 1930s, over 1,700,000 cars were licensed in Britain. The garage became a feature of the middle-class home. Petrol-filling and service stations began to proliferate and grow in size. With the increase in traffic, multi-purpose buildings which combined car parks with petrol filling and servicing facilities became common.

The new phenomenon of traffic congestion demanded new roads, capable of coping with the vehicles now inside our cities. Liverpool's Mersey Tunnel, begun in 1925, is an early modern traffic route as well as an under-river link with Birkenhead. Liverpool also gained its first 'skyscraper', St George's Ventilation Tower, as a result of the tunnel's construction.

As private transport filled the roads, public transport also increased at first. The bus and coach systems that emerged in the first quarter of the century linked most parts of the country. With the development of the services came new coach stations that could vary in size from the Windsor Green Line Station to the grand Victoria Coach Station, London. Opposite Victoria Coach Station, in Buckingham Palace Road, stands a terminal designed to be a prelude to a rather different form of travel: built in 1939 as the Imperial Airways Empire Terminal, this was the rallying point for passengers to Europe and India and, later for passenger flights to the United States. In the Second

World War the aeroplane was developed to a point where its eventual domination of our external transport systems became possible.

Travel by air had its tremulous beginning as far back as 1903 when the Wright Brothers made their first flight in a heavier-than-air machine. In 1912, after the sinking of the *Titanic, The Graphic* wistfully reflected, 'If only we could fly the Atlantic! One way by which the iceberg danger would be avoided!' The crossing was achieved in 1919 by Alcock and Brown, but at that stage it remained safer to travel by sea or by airship. The airship era has left us with a major pair of buildings, the airship hangars at Cardington, Bedfordshire, in which the R100 and R101 were constructed.

The 1920s saw the infant airlines struggle for existence. Flying clubs had already been formed by that time and, as in the early days of the motor car, a very wealthy few actually owned 'planes' for private use. Gradually aerodromes appeared throughout the country. Their early needs were perhaps a few hundred yards of level firm ground, a windsock and some enclosed buildings for use as offices. These last became more sophisticated in the 1930s. The earliest flying ground was at Brooklands in the middle of the motor circuit, where flights began as early as 1907/8. Various hangars were built in the succeeding years, but it was not until 1932 that the Brooklands Aero Clubhouse, with its distinctive style, was built. It was the most up-to-date aerodrome building in the country. Brooklands and the contemporary aerodrome at Heston both catered largely for private flying, so it is not surprising that they both look like country clubs. Heston, however, was a clear advance on Brooklands in that its planes could take off and land on a smooth non-skid surface rather than Brookland's grassy field. Heston was also the first 'airpark' to be filled with wireless telephonic apparatus with a range of 300 miles. At a time when aerodromes were not properly equipped for night flying, flood lighting, which was switched on from the control tower, was also introduced at Heston.

Experience gained from the building of Heston influenced the design of the attractive airport at Shoreham in Sussex, which was built in 1936. This airport catered for private flying in the main, and continues to do so to this day with very little change in the original building.

In the mid and late 1930s, airports became very interesting indeed. Gatwick Airport of 1936 still excites admiration with its 'design of the future' which was intended to be highly practical. The low elevation reduced obstruction to aircraft, while the circular form made it a clear focal point from the air. The advantages in satisfactory circulation and control of passengers and planes were considerable. The circular control room, with its continuous wall of glass, gave a perfect view of air traffic. Passengers had the additional comfort of the shelter provided by radial corridors that ran out on tracks from the building to the waiting planes.

Jersey Airport, completed in 1937, proved more conventional in appearance but the aeronautical theme could be traced in its ground-plan. The hangars extended backwards like the wings of a swallow in flight. Novel features included the spacious public promenade decks and the weighing hall for outgoing passengers.

The last important airport to be built in England before the Second World War was the Birmingham (Elmdon) Airport in 1939. It catered for direct air connection with the Continent. One might deduce from its 'winged' appearance that it was about to take off itself! In fact these 'wings' were balanced cantilevers permitting passengers and freight to be loaded and unloaded entirely under cover. The large hangar at one side of the building further simplified air traffic movement.

The confidence of the airlines in the commercial prospects of air travel is reflected in the fact that all the 1930s airports mentioned above were designed so that they could be extended at a later date. As we all know, subsequent events have more than justified their confidence.

Airports were not unique in having a highly individual appearance. Other new types of building could be equally striking. The great power stations of the 1930s such as Battersea and Fulham, supplying power to large parts of London, dominated the skyline. They have been likened to great ships with their tall smokestacks and cavernous turbine halls. The needs of ships themselves occasioned new buildings, such as Vickers Supermarine Works in Southampton (built 1937) with its vast counterbalanced door on the wharf.

Some new buildings can be accounted for by social changes. Working conditions improved after the First World War, and many new factories boasted better facilities. The Hoover Factory's handsome canteen building is a case in point. Another improvement in social conditions was in general health standards. Strenuous efforts were made to achieve it in the 1930s and one major result was the provision of health centres like that at Finsbury. Here the various medical services, previously scattered over the borough, were centralized in

one building and were available at about one shilling per week per family. Flexibility was a keynote in the design, anticipating advances in medical techniques and equipment. All the clinics were on the ground floor, to the patients' benefit. A particular refinement was the absence of dark corridors and courtyards; instead of the traditional hospital gloom, the maximum of sunlight and cross-ventilation prevailed. This emphasis on light and air in public buildings had its roots in the reforms of Florence Nightingale, but the twentieth century has seen it pushed possibly to its limits. There was a considerable development of the theme in the 1930s. Entire areas of wall were then 'built' in glass, uniting the inner space with the great outdoors.

Also in the thirties, there was a near obsession with a cult of the open air. Sunbathing and swimming became increasingly popular, and sun patios, lidos and open-air swimming-pools became common. Simultaneously covered pools were built which enabled far more people to swim all the year round than those who had used the municipal baths of late Victorian England.

Although the South Coast remained a popular holiday area, it had to compete with the lure of an increasingly accessible Europe. The resorts therefore launched a massive reinvestment programme. Pleasure palaces were one result. Two of the most successful were Dreamland in Margate and the De la Warr Pavilion in Bexhill. Both offered a variety of facilities, but Dreamland was more like a fairground while the De la Warr Pavilion had a more cultural basis. Instigated by the Earl De la Warr, then Mayor of Bexhill, the pavilion provided in one building a repertory theatre, restaurant, rooms for its own band and *thés dansants*,

a small auditorium for recitals and talks, a reading-room, and a sun lounge leading to a sundeck. The high-minded theme of this social experiment was supposed to suggest to future generations ways of employing their leisure and to help the idea of modern architecture penetrate the life of contemporary society. Certainly it has made its mark.

The theme of leisure was an element of the Earl's Court Exhibition Hall, built in 1937. While this Hall has often served commercial purposes, it has also offered the public the opportunity to see the latest developments in almost anything that man can make. The façade brilliantly announces the building, and has something of the quality of a cinema proscenium. The cinema building has been a more widespread form of entertainment hall. Very much a new type of building of this century's first three decades, the cinema was created for a film industry that was in fact born in the very last years of the nineteenth century. In the early days film was taken from music hall to fairground, from rented hall to converted shop. These earliest venues were known as 'penny-gaffs', were usually uncomfortable and frequently dangerous, for early film often exploded. A number of well-publicized fires precipitated the introduction of the Cinematographic Act of 1909, which imposed various safety standards. This Act, and the growing demand for film entertainment, made it clear that a special sort of building would be necessary. The first purpose-built cinemas appeared at the end of the first decade of the century. By 1910, the London County Council had granted two hundred licences for cinematographic theatres; in Manchester there were more cinemas per person than in any other part of the country. Cinemas began to offer comfort and respectability, an appropriate setting for a 'night out'. They were richly decorated in marble and plush, and palms and ferns enhanced the effect. Proper flap-back armchairs replaced the wooden benches of early days. Cinemas were then lit by electricity, and in the early days low-level illumination, known as 'morality lighting', remained throughout the performance. The entertainment gradually shed its less respectable origins and further improved its image during the First World War. Then Britain followed the events of the War as filmed by Pathé News and sought diversion during those four grim years in the romantic melodramas and slapstick routines of the period.

After the War, many cinemas were built and certain adaptations began to affect their appearance. The best seats were at the back to reduce the distortion of the picture; a cinema architect had to forget rectangular walls and high balconies and instead plan with projection and vision lines in mind. The cinema as a type of building developed a curved fan-shape in plan. The surface of the interior had also to be considered for acoustic qualities following the commercial advent of the 'talkies' in 1927 with Al Jolson's *The Jazz Singer*. The era of the super cinema had dawned.

Throughout the 1930s many of the country's finest cinemas were built. Great trouble was taken over their interiors, which could vary from distinctive *moderne* to a fantasy world of pastiche. A prelude to the film itself was the playing of the cinema organ, an adjunct which has now become almost extinct.

The films of the time were mostly imported from America, but in the 1930s the British film industry caught up. One result was the magnificent set of studios built at Denham, Buckinghamshire, in 1936 for London Film Productions. The other great studios of the period were those of the BBC, built in 1931. Radio broadcasting began in 1922 and the construction of Broadcasting House reflected its immediate and widespread success. The BBC also began experimenting with the newly invented television system; Broadcasting House contained a small television studio, but programmes were ultimately broadcast from Alexandra Palace, London, from 1936 onwards. The cinema's competitor and immediate successor had quietly arrived.

We can already see the twentieth century as an age when great advances in communication have been achieved. Most of the buildings illustrated here have been involved in one way or another in the early phases of new methods of communication. Whether for the transport of man or the transmission of his messages, we can see them as built for their age and representative of it. Though many serve us still, and are part of our everyday surroundings, the perspective of the last forty or fifty years is already beginning to define some as historical monuments in much the same sense as we regard a Georgian toll-house or a Roman amphitheatre.

BROOKLANDS MOTOR CIRCUIT, WALTON AND WEYBRIDGE, SURREY.
Brooklands Motor Circuit, the first of its kind in Britain, was the creation of
the civil engineer H. F. Locke King. It was completed in 1907. Racing was last
held here in 1939. The recently formed Brooklands Society keeps part of the
track in recognizable condition.

1 This photograph shows part of the track rising to the saucer rim at the
  back. The clubhouse on the left was destined to serve as Barnes Wallis's
  research station during the Second World War. Bedford Lemere, 1927.

2 The opening day parade, led by Mr and Mrs Locke King in a 70 hp Itala,
  developed from a sedate procession into a rip-roaring race. Other drivers
  included C. S. Rolls and Warwick Wright whose Darracq touched 85 mph.
  Photographer unknown, 1907. Copyright Elmbridge Borough Council.

3 (*opposite, above*) MITCHELL MOTORS, WARDOUR STREET, LONDON.
This garage was built *c* 1907. It was fitted with a motor-car lift, which helped to solve some of the problems of the limited space available in central London. In later and larger garages, circular ramps admitted cars to upper floors. Bedford Lemere, 1907.

4 (*opposite, below*) MACY'S GARAGE, BALDERTON STREET, LONDON.
Macy's Garage was completed in 1926. The architects were Wimperis and Simpson. Its situation just off Oxford Street ensured a brisk trade. In common with many garages of the 1920s, Macy's was given a faintly classical façade. It is now used by the Ford Motor Company. Bedford Lemere, 1927.

5 DARRACQ'S MOTORCAR SHOWROOM, NEW BOND STREET, LONDON.
R. Frank Atkinson designed this showroom for the Paris-based firm of Darracq Motorcar Manufacturers in 1914. He created a subdued interior which allowed the vehicles to be seen at their best. He could not control the shape of the site, however, which explains the slightly cramped system of display afforded by the long narrow showroom. Forty years after this photograph was taken, a 1904 Darracq graced the famous film *Genevieve*. Bedford Lemere, 1914.

6 (*overleaf*) MICHELIN TYRE COMPANY BUILDING, FULHAM ROAD, LONDON.
The Michelin building was designed by F. Espinasse. It was begun in 1905 and further extended in 1910. The Company's merchandise was wittily advertised by the architectural motifs on the motoring theme: cupolas resembling piles of tyres, motor-car wheels in the pediments and tiled illustrations of cars and bicycles decorating the pillars. Even though the Michelin Man no longer adorns the top of the main window, his origins are clearly implicit in the rest of the décor that survives. Bedford Lemere, 1910.

7 (*opposite, above*) BLUEBIRD GARAGE, 330–340 KING'S ROAD, LONDON.
This garage was built in 1924 for the Bluebird Motor Company. It was said to be the largest in Europe when new. Its 50,000 square feet had room for 300 cars; a further 7,000 square feet were given over to workshops. Two buildings on either side of the garage contained segregated lounges and writing rooms for ladies, owner occupiers and chauffeurs. The garage was open day and night. It was fitted with a large number of petrol pumps as well as 60 tyre inflation points.
The building has latterly been in use as an ambulance station. Bedford Lemere, 1928.

8 (*opposite, below*) SHELLMEX GARAGE, FULHAM, LONDON.
This was a large servicing station built in the early 1920s with room for a great variety of vehicles as well as pieces of equipment like the motor-repair stand shown in the foreground. The extensive skylights ensured the maximum of natural daylight. Notices to the staff begged them not to smoke and to 'Be Clean'. Bedford Lemere, 1926.

9 GOLLY'S GARAGE, EARL'S COURT ROAD, LONDON.
This garage was built about 1935. Its ground floor was faced in tiles, which were easy to clean. The staff were sheltered by the cantilevered canopy, a twentieth-century variation of the old *porte-cochère*. Skylights were inserted into the canopy.
   The garage is now derelict. Herbert Felton, *c* 1935. Copyright *The Architect & Building News* (B. W. S. Publishing).

STEPNEY CARRIER COMPANY GARAGE, 94–100 ST JOHN STREET, LONDON.

This garage was completed in 1935 to the design of the architects Milner and Craze. It was incorporated within the business office building, which also housed on an upper floor the Company's 'box carriers' where they could be repaired separately. As well as a car-lift, the garage also had a turntable and washes.

10 (*opposite*) Precautions against fire necessitated the deep recess running through the entire height of the building as well as the use of fireproof construction materials throughout. Herbert Felton, 1935.

11 The photograph shows the interior of the garage and filling station. Herbert Felton, 1935.

12 THE DAIMLER CAR HIRE GARAGE, HERBRAND STREET, LONDON.

Wallis Gilbert and Partners designed the Daimler Car Hire Garage in 1931. It stored Daimler-owned cars on its upper floors, while the basement was used as a car park for privately-owned cars. Up to 500 cars in all could be parked. The design provided for the addition of an extra floor. The ramp, giving access to the upper floors, took up comparatively little of the site area. The private owners' garage was equipped with a waiting-room, attendant's office, lavatories and telephones. Each floor had an electrically operated pressure washing plant for the cars. The garage was well lit, both naturally and artificially. Herbert Felton, 1931. Copyright *The Architect and Building News* (B. W. S. Publishing)

OLYMPIA GARAGE, KENSINGTON, LONDON.
This garage, completed in 1937 to the design of Joseph Emberton, comprised eleven mezzanine floors, holding 1,000 cars.

13 The exterior had two garage entrances leading directly to ramps at either end of the building. Herbert Felton, 1937, Copyright *The Architect and Building News* (B. W. S. Publishing).

14 (*opposite, above*) The fifth floor; each floor was lit by an unbroken row of windows. The columns supporting the floors were protected by substantial curbs. Herbert Felton, 1937. Copyright *The Architect and Building News* (B. W. S. Publishing).

15 (*opposite, below*) One of the two ramps, which were designed to give the easiest gradient from one floor to another. They were eight feet high with a constant superelevation of five inches on the outside of each ramp to assist the steering of the cars. Herbert Felton, 1937. Copyright *The Architect and Building News* (B. W. S. Publishing).

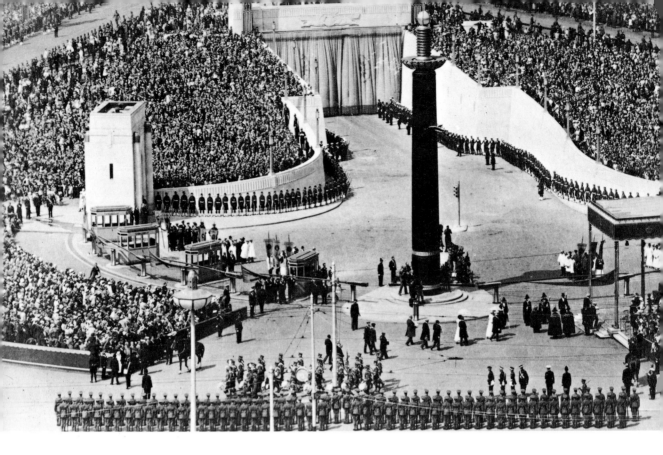

MERSEY TUNNEL, LIVERPOOL, MERSEYSIDE.
The engineers Sir Basil Mott and J. A. Brodie collaborated on the design of the Mersey Tunnel, which was begun in 1925. Herbert J. Rowse was appointed architect in 1931.

16 The lodges at this entrance were built with French 1925 *moderne* details and with Egyptian touches, especially the fluted column-like buttresses. This photograph shows the inauguration of the tunnel by T. M. King George V and Queen Mary in 1934. F. G. Thomas, 1934.

17 The interior of the Mersey Tunnel was electrically lit throughout. The road was fitted with the newly invented cat's-eyes and there were fire points at regular intervals along the route. Stewart Bale, 1934.

19 GREEN LINE COACHING STATION, WINDSOR, BERKSHIRE.
Wallis Gilbert and Partners designed this coaching station for the Green
Line in 1933. It combined all the facilities of a coach station with the
equipment of a first-class garage, accommodating sixty coaches and buses.
Emphasis was put on the need for speedy circulation of the coaches and
buses. Herbert Felton, 1933. Copyright *The Architect and Building News*
(B. W. S. Publishing).

20 VICTORIA COACH STATION, BUCKINGHAM PALACE ROAD,
LONDON.
The Victoria Coach Station was designed by Wallis Gilbert and Partners
and completed in 1932. It was the first really large motor-coach station to
be built in England. Its passenger facilities were praised for their warmth,
light, cheerfulness and draught-free qualities. It was also deemed
impossible to get lost. Latter-day visitors might disagree on both these
counts. The coach station remains in use. Herbert Felton, 1932.

18 (*previous page*) ST GEORGE'S
VENTILATION TOWER, LIVERPOOL,
MERSEYSIDE.
Herbert J. Rowse and Sir Basil Mott
collaborated on the design of the premier
ventilation tower over the Mersey Tunnel.
It was completed in 1934. It has much of
the character of a contemporary American
skyscraper. It was decorated in a 'jazz
moderne' style, and was given giant
reeded blank windows. Herbert Felton,
1935. Copyright *The Architect and Building
News* (B. W. S. Publishing).

21 (*opposite*) IMPERIAL AIRWAYS EMPIRE
TERMINAL, BUCKINGHAM PALACE
ROAD, LONDON
The Empire Terminal was designed by
A. Lakeman and built in 1939. The motif
of the skyscraper, pointing to the clouds,
is perhaps fitting for an air terminal. The
site was chosen for its direct access to
Victoria Station, allowing passengers to
board a train for Southampton, where the
flying boat awaited them. Passengers for
Continental routes boarded a coach from
the terminal to the airport. At a time
when the 'all up' weight of an aircraft
was more important than now, the design
of part of the terminal showed great tact.
Sections of the floor, where passengers
stood to check in, concealed a set of
scales so that people of ample proportions
should never be called upon to clamber
aboard a weighing machine in full view of
their fellow travellers. The passenger
check-in facility was finally closed in
November 1980. The ticket office and
medical centre remain. J. Stone, *c* 1946.

22 AIRSHIP HANGARS, CARDINGTON, BEDFORDSHIRE.
These were originally built in 1917 for Short Brothers. One of the hangars was lengthened to permit construction of the R100 in 1927. In the same year the other hangar was rebuilt to accommodate the construction of the R101. The RAF took both hangars over in 1936 and later they were used as the HQ of London's Balloon Barrage Manufacture. Later still they were used by British Aerospace. They are currently in use again for airship construction. F. R. Winstone, *c* 1936.

BROOKLANDS AERODROME, WALTON AND WEYBRIDGE, SURREY.
The clubhouse was designed by G. Dawbarn and completed in 1932. Its roofs were used as terraces for spectators. Aeroplanes were monitored from the control room at the top of the tower.

23 (*opposite, below*) The aerodrome and its flying school were advertised to the airborne by the large letters painted on the roof of the big 1920s hangar behind the clubhouse. Aeroplanes landed on a grass field and taxied up to a small spear-shaped concrete apron along which passengers would walk to embark. G. F. and M. I. Webb, 1932.

24 The clubhouse entrance was on the other side. Hopefully the public will once again enter the clubhouse if plans to convert it into a museum of aviation are realized. G. F. and M. I. Webb, 1932.

HESTON AIRPORT, HOUNSLOW, GREATER LONDON.
Heston's clubhouse and control tower were completed in 1929 to the design of L. M. Austin and H. F. Murrell. Heston gained a permanent place in history when the Prime Minister, Neville Chamberlain, returned here after his final meeting with Adolf Hitler in Munich, in October 1938.

25 (*previous spread, inset*) The clubhouse and control tower were not particularly distinguished in appearance apart from the control room with its projecting balcony which resembled the bridge of a ship. This building was demolished in 1978. Herbert Felton, 1929. Copyright *The Architect and Building News* (B. W. S. Publishing).

26 (*previous spread*) This hangar was one of two built for Heston by A. Jackamann in 1929. One contained school and taxi-machines. The other (illustrated) was the 'lock-up' hangar for privately-owned planes. Its aerodynamic shape was dictated by the need for a side-to-side span so that the whole of the front facing the aerodrome could be covered by one large folding door, 18 feet high. This hangar has been altered but remains in use. Herbert Felton, 1929. Copyright *The Architect and Building News* (B. W. S. Publishing).

GATWICK AIRPORT, CRAWLEY, WEST SUSSEX.
Gatwick Airport was designed by Hoar, Marlow and Lovett and completed in 1936. Its circular shape, which still evokes thoughts of the future, or the flying saucer, was a change from other airport buildings described at the time as being based on railway stations or dock buildings. Gatwick's scheme of concentric circles was pierced by five radial corridors, giving on to 'tunnels' that ran out on tracks in the concrete apron to the waiting planes. This building remains in use near the new airport built in the 1960s.

27 (*opposite*) Interior. The passenger concourse had shops on the left and the administrative counter on the right. The top lighting was an important feature. Herbert Felton, 1936. Copyright *The Architect and Building News* (B. W. S. Publishing).

28 The exterior of the control tower, which projected above the main building. The tower consisted of a self-supporting circular slab roof and ring of windows in a wood-frame. This allowed unbroken viewing. Herbert Felton, 1936. Copyright *The Architect and Building News* (B. W. S. Publishing).

29 (*overleaf, inset*) Detail of tunnel on track. Herbert Felton, 1936. Copyright *The Architect and Building News* (B. W. S. Publishing);

30 (*overleaf*) Exterior. Herbert Felton, 1936. Copyright *The Architect and Building News* (B. W. S. Publishing).

JERSEY AIRPORT, CHANNEL ISLANDS.
Jersey Airport was designed by Norman and
Dawbarn and completed in 1937. It
combined, in one wide building, two
hangars, passenger facilities, airport offices
and a control tower. A large apron
surrounded the building.

31 Exterior, taken from the landing ground.
Herbert Felton, 1937. Copyright *The
Architect and Building News* (B. W. S.
Publishing).

32 The control tower. Airport offices were on
the third floor, with the control room on
the floor above. The lower floors were
given over to passenger facilities. Herbert
Felton, 1937. Copyright *The Architect and
Building News* (B. W. S. Publishing).

33 The interior of the control room. Herbert Felton, 1937. Copyright *The Architect and Building News* (B. W. S. Publishing)

34 Weighing room for embarking passengers. Herbert Felton, 1937. Copyright *The Architect and Building News* (B. W. S. Publishing).

35 This public promenade overlooked Hangar No. 2. Passengers and spectators could sit here and watch arrivals and departures. Deck chairs and snacks were available. Herbert Felton, 1937. Copyright *The Architect and Building News* (B. W. S. Publishing).

36 (*overleaf, inset*) Hangar No. 1, showing the main doors and apron. Herbert Felton, 1937. Copyright *The Architect and Building News* (B. W. S. Publishing).

37 (*overleaf*) Interior of a hangar with a collection of Dragon Rapides. Herbert Felton, 1937. Copyright *The Architect and Building News* (B. W. S. Publishing).

38 SHOREHAM AIRPORT, SHOREHAM-BY-SEA, WEST SUSSEX.
Shoreham Airport was completed in 1936 to the design of Stavers H. Tiltman, who worked with James Bodell and consultants from Heston Airport. The top floor of the airport building was allocated to air traffic control and the floors below were given over to administrative offices, a restaurant and bar, and a customs hall. These retain much of their original decoration, while the control room still has its Aldis Lamp which was used to signal to the planes before the days of radio contact. Britain's first cargo flight was from Shoreham Airport. The Royal Canadian Air Force was based there during the Second World War. It is now Britain's oldest surviving licensed airport. H. E. S. Simmons, 1937.

BIRMINGHAM (ELMDON) AIRPORT, BICKENHILL, WEST MIDLANDS.
Birmingham Airport was built in 1939 by Norman and Dawbarn in conjunction with Herbert I. Manzoni, the Birmingham City Engineer Surveyor. It was intended to be used for flights to the Continent as well as by flying schools and clubs. It remains in use.

39 The entrance front, from the car park. A structure with wings (they are cantilevered canopies) can be seen as appropriate for an airport. A pair of delicate spiral staircases led to a balcony. Herbert Felton, 1939. Copyright *The Architect and Building News* (B. S. W. Publishing).

40 The aircraft hangar was on a fairly large scale for its time and was fitted with huge sliding doors. It was shared by Birmingham Corporation, the Midlands Aero Club, formed in 1909 and, prophetically, the RAF Volunteer Reserves. Herbert Felton, 1939. Copyright *The Architect and Building News* (B. W. S. Publishing).

41 (*opposite*) The circular control tower was above three semi-circular open galleries where passengers could view proceedings while taking tea. Herbert Felton, 1939. Copyright *The Architect and Building News* (B. W. S. Publishing).

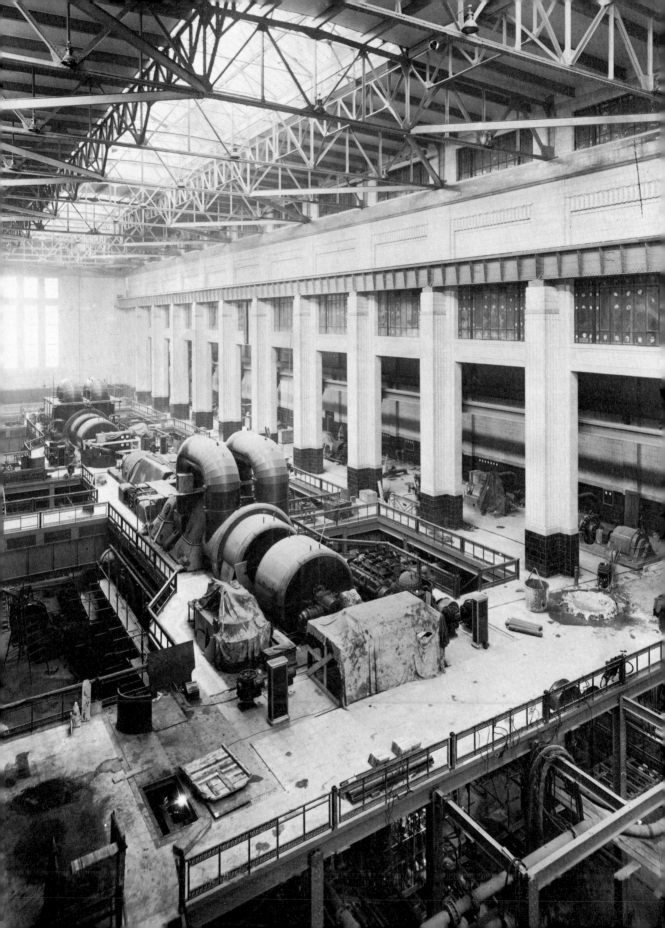

42 (*opposite*) BATTERSEA POWER STATION, LONDON.
The station had several turbine halls in which the power for central London was generated. This awe-inspiring room recalls the engine room of a great ocean liner. The photograph shows it nearing completion. Herbert Felton, 1932. Copyright *The Architect and Building News* (B. W. S. Publishing).

43 Battersea Power Station was built in two stages, the first half being begun in 1929 and completed in 1934. The whole building had to wait until 1955 to be finished. It was designed by Halliday and Agate, with additional exterior work by Sir Giles Gilbert Scott. It is to close in 1983. It was listed in 1980, but its future is not clear. Herbert Felton, 1932. Copyright *The Architect and Building News* (B. W. S. Publishing).

44 FULHAM POWER STATION, LONDON.
This was designed by G. E. Baker and built in 1936. It was planned as the largest municipally-owned generating plant in the country. It is still in use. Herbert Felton, 1936. Copyright *The Architect and Building News* (B. W. S. Publishing).

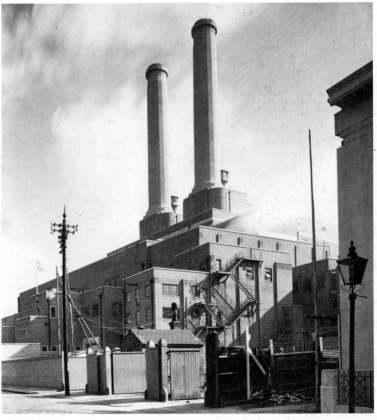

45 (*opposite*) VICKERS SUPERMARINE WORKS, SOUTHAMPTON, HAMPSHIRE.
The Vickers Supermarine Works was built in 1936–7 to the design of the well-known architect and interior designer, Oliver P. Bernard. This remarkable vast rectractable steel door was supplied by Hawkes and Snow Limited. It has been echoed countless times on a much smaller scale by our modern domestic garage doors. The works gave on to a dock for loading. Herbert Felton, 1937. Copyright *The Architect and Building News* (B. W. S. Publishing).

46 CANTEEN BUILDING, HOOVER FACTORY, WESTERN AVENUE, LONDON.
Wallis Gilbert and Partners designed the Hoover Factory and its canteen building in 1932–5. The factory was remarkable for its modern facilities and its individual appearance. It has certainly excited comment over the years. For example, in 1951 Pevsner found it 'perhaps the most offensive of the modernistic atrocities along this road of typical by-pass factories'. Nonetheless, the Hoover Factory possesses a distinctive 'factory' style and its importance has been highlighted by the recent demolition of the equally interesting Firestone Factory. Both these factories were provided with large areas of lawn and flower bedding, part of the garden-city ideal of enhancing the working conditions and recreation of the labour force. The Hoover Factory was listed in 1980. Herbert Felton, *c* 1938.

FINSBURY HEALTH CENTRE, ISLINGTON, LONDON.
The Finsbury Health Centre was built in 1938 to the design of Tecton and Berthold Lubetkin. It represented a new beginning in the borough's medical services, an innovation exemplified in the design of the building. It is no longer in pristine condition.

47 (*overleaf*) The front elevation was faced in glass bricks. There was a sun balcony on the first floor upon which were plants and shrubs. J. Scheerboom, *c* 1958.

48 (*overleaf, inset*) The Disinfection Station entrance. Clinics and offices were kept completely separate from a mortuary and other necessarily 'unclean' parts of the centre. The small hopper units of the windows allowed variable ventilation controlled in connection with the mechanical extract ventilation system. Herbert Felton, 1939. Copyright *The Architect and Building News* (B. S. W. Publishing).

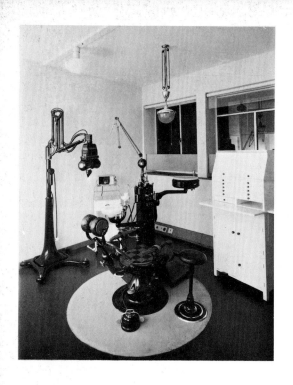

49 The Dental Clinic fitted with all the latest equipment. This photograph could almost be a work of surrealist art. Herbert Felton, 1939. Copyright *The Architect and Building News* (B. W. S. Publishing).

50 This staircase had copperized mesh fixed to vertical tubes carrying wiring to the light fittings. The handrail was covered in plastic. At the head and to the left of this staircase was the entrance to the reception house where families were accommodated while their own houses were disinfected. Herbert Felton, 1939. Copyright *The Architect and Building News* (B. W. S. Publishing).

51 The 'Electrical Treatment' Clinic. It had facilities for private treatment in addition to its general services. The Clinic was ventilated by a mechanical air extraction system. The chairs are the work of Alvar Aalto and would have been considered the very latest thing. Herbert Felton, 1939. Copyright *The Architect and Building News* (B. W. S. Publishing).

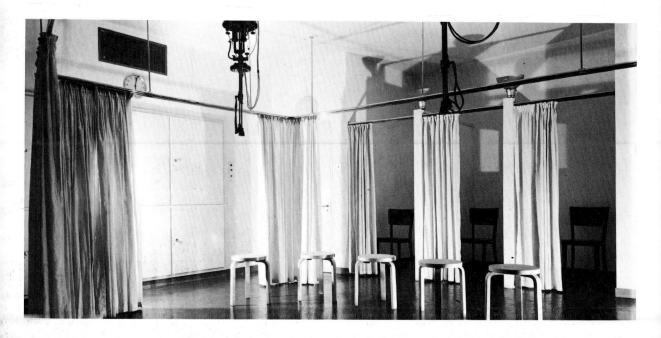

52 (*previous page*) DE LA WARR PAVILION, BEXHILL, EAST SUSSEX.
The De la Warr Pavilion was designed by Mendelsohn and Chermayeff and completed in 1935. It incorporated large amounts of sheet glass, in particular around the spiral staircase overlooking the sea. It is still a great pleasure to use this dramatic staircase on a fine day when the effect is one of being almost entirely surrounded by sea and sunlight. Herbert Felton, 1935. Copyright *The Architect and Building News* (B. W. S. Publishing).

53 NO. 2, SOUTH PARADE, EALING, LONDON.
The sun-patio was a feature widely used in the 1930s, owing a little to Continental and American influence. Bitter experience still reminds us that the British open-air romance is not always ideally served by its climate. Herbert Felton, *c* 1939. Copyright *The Architect and Building News* (B. W. S. Publishing).

54 RESERVOIR LIDO, RUISLIP, LONDON.
This lido was built for the Grand Union Canal Company in 1936 by Thomas H. Mawson and Son. It was projected as one of the first of many lidos to be distributed over a wide area on extensive reservoirs belonging to the company. The central portion contained a restaurant, dance floor and terrace; wings contained changing rooms. There were spacious lawns, tennis courts and also a car park for 250 cars. Herbert Felton, 1936. Copyright *The Architect and Building News* (B. W. S. Publishing).

55 ROEHAMPTON SWIMMING POOL, LONDON.
This pool was built in 1934 to the design of George W. Smith. Public bathing in England can be traced back to the Romans, but the open-air swimming pool is very much a twentieth-century development reflecting the changes in attitudes to health as well as modesty in dress. Herbert Felton, 1934. Copyright *The Architect and Building News* (B. W. S. Publishing).

SHOWBOAT LIDO, MAIDENHEAD, BERKSHIRE.

The 'Showboat' was built in 1933 to the design of E. Norman Bailey and D. C. Wadhwa. This 'roadhouse' was a new type of building which emerged in the inter-war years as a result of the rise in popularity of the motor car. It was seen as the answer to motorists' prayers: a retreat from the dusty torments of the road.

56 Its cheerful exterior was painted in eau-de-nil and flesh pink, enclosing a restaurant, ballroom, clubroom and bar, and providing the backdrop to tea and sunbathing terraces and a large swimming-pool. Herbert Felton, 1933. Copyright *The Architect and Building News* (B. W. S. Publishing).

57 Swimming pool. The design of the pool, and indeed the whole road-house, owed much to the architect's experience of contemporary continental bathing pools. With its sunny terraces and verdant surroundings, it must have been a delightful place to spend a fine afternoon. Herbert Felton, 1933. Copyright *The Architect and Building News* (B. W. S. Publishing).

EMPIRE SWIMMING-POOL, WEMBLEY, LONDON.

This huge building was designed by O. Williams and completed in 1934. Williams' imaginative and confident use of massive exterior counterweights created a building which leaves an overwhelming impression.

58 (*overleaf, inset*) Interior. This was thought to be the largest pool in the world when it was built. The concrete cantilevered roof has a span of 236 feet. Herbert Felton, 1934. Copyright *The Architect and Building News* (B. W. S. Publishing).

59 (*overleaf*) Exterior. Herbert Felton, 1934. Copyright *The Architect and Buildings News* (B. W. S. Publishing).

DE LA WARR PAVILION, BEXHILL, EAST SUSSEX.
The construction of the De la Warr Pavilion followed a controversial competition which was won by Mendelsohn and Chermayeff. The Pavilion was completed in 1935. Its appearance and serious purpose represent changes from the traditional seaside building.

   The Pavilion numbered among its attractions an auditorium, doubling as a cinema, a sun lounge and reading-room.

60 (*opposite*) Close-up of the glass bay containing the spiral staircase leading to the lounge and sun roof. Herbert Felton, 1937. Copyright *The Architect and Building News* (B. W. S. Publishing).

61 (*opposite, inset*) Exterior. Herbert Felton, 1935. Copyright *The Architect and Building News* (B. W. S. Publishing).

62 Auditorium. The moulded plaster ceiling was designed to improve acoustics. Herbert Felton, 1935. Copyright *The Architect and Building News* (B. W. S. Publishing).

63 (*overleaf*) Sun lounge and reading-room. This was a further example of the Pavilion's cultural purpose. Apart from its supposed benefits to health, the sun lounge was a reminder of the sort of leisure to be found on an ocean liner. Many new buildings of the 1930s embodied the nautical ethos of the period. Herbert Felton, 1935. Copyright *The Architect and Building News* (B. W. S. Publishing).

DREAMLAND, MARGATE, KENT.
Dreamland was designed by Iles, Leathart, and Granger and built in 1934.

64 The exterior from the west. This is almost a fusion of cinema and High Street shop. The publicity frames on the tower, advertising the current programme, were illuminated at night, and the effect was particularly impressive when seen from the sea. Herbert Felton, *c* 1934. Copyright *The Architect and Building News* (B. W. S. Publishing).

65 A view of part of the funfair, showing the miniature railway and steel-framed concrete buffet building. Herbert Felton, *c* 1934. Copyright *The Architect and Building News* (B. W. S. Publishing).

EARL'S COURT EXHIBITION BUILDING,
LONDON.
The Earl's Court complex of exhibition halls
was designed by C. Howard Crane and
Partners and built in 1937. It was the first
building in London designed to cater solely
for year-round commercial exhibitions. Its
vast spaces included a double-tier car park
for 2,000 cars. Recently the building has been
superseded by the Birmingham Trade
Centre.

66 The front of the building. The main
entrance façades are of reinforced
concrete on a mammoth frame. Herbert
Felton, 1937. Copyright Architectural
Press.

67 Interior of one of the exhibition halls,
nearing completion. The massive air-
conditioning machinery leaves an
impression of something from the
contemporary film of H. G. Wells' novel
The War of the Worlds. Herbert Felton,
1937. Copyright Architectural Press.

68 PYKES CINEMATOGRAPH THEATRE, BALHAM, LONDON.

Pykes Cinematograph Theatre was built in 1911 for the ACT Circuit. Filmgoers were enticed to this cinema, now demolished, to see such forthcoming films as *Judith of Bethulia* 'in four parts', extravagantly advertised as 'the world's greatest film' and 'the limit of the Kinematographic Art'. In 1915 few, apart from the visionaries, can have guessed just how far the medium of film would advance. Bedford Lemere, 1915.

163 E. A. OWEN LTD 163
BOOKS, STATIONERY, FANCY & LEATHER GOODS

FROM 2 TO CONTINUOUS
10 30 DAILY PERFORMANCE

PICTURE HOUSE

THE PICTURE HOUSE

69 (*opposite*) THE PICTURE HOUSE, LIVERPOOL, MERSEYSIDE.
The Picture House was built in 1912. Its imposing and sizeable façade was an outward symbol of the new-found success of the cinema. From 2 pm until 10.30 pm, the cinema offered a continuous daily programme, including early 'sex films'. The Picture House has recently found a new role as the Shrine of the Blessed Sacrament. Bedford Lemere, 1912.

70 CINEMATOGRAPHIC THEATRE, 583 FULHAM ROAD, LONDON.
This small cinema, built *c* 1914, shared space with a surveyor's office. It appears to hark back to the old 'penny-gaff' although it would have been more advanced. Bedford Lemere, 1915.

71 BIRMINGHAM CINEMA, BIRMINGHAM, WEST MIDLANDS.
The Birmingham Cinema was built *c* 1911. The interior, with its plush seats and elaborate plasterwork, recalls the Victorian or Edwardian theatre. The blank screen, however, instantly gives this 'theatre' a new dimension, an impression of waiting to look through a 'window' into another world. Bedford Lemere, 1911.

72 WALPOLE PICTURE THEATRE, EALING, LONDON.
The Walpole Picture Theatre was originally built as a roller-skating rink *c* 1900 and converted to a cinema in 1912. This photograph shows its 'Big Screen'. The building has latterly been used as a carpet shop and is shortly to be demolished. Bedford Lemere, *c* 1912.

73 KENTISH TOWN PALACE CINEMA,
LONDON.

The early cinemas were long box-like
shapes, not ideally designed for their
purpose. This cinema, built *c* 1912, shows
no sign of the fan-shape plan that was
later to evolve. There were, however, two
large exits, doubtless enforced by the
Cinematographic Act of 1909. Bedford
Lemere, 1913.

74 RIALTO CINEMA, MAIDENHEAD, BERKSHIRE.
The Rialto was built *c* 1926. A subdued classical décor was chosen for its interior, the latter showing signs of development towards the 'fan-shaped' auditorium. Bedford Lemere, 1926.

75 KENSINGTON KINEMA, KENSINGTON HIGH STREET, LONDON.
The Kensington Kinema was designed by Leathart and Granger and completed in 1926. It sat 2,300 people. It won critical and public praise for its design and in particular for the fine neo-classical exterior. This has suffered crude additions which mar its original elegance. The imposing entrance has been altered, to its detriment, and the large urns on their pedestals have disappeared. The Kensington Kinema has been renamed the Odeon. Bedford Lemere, 1926.

GAUMONT PALACE, WOLVERHAMPTON, WEST MIDLANDS.
The Gaumont Palace was designed by W. E. Trent and built in 1932.

76 Exterior. The architect managed to overcome the difficulties of a corner site while taking advantage of the curve of the road to provide the desired fan-shape for the cinema. Herbert Felton, 1934. Copyright *Architectural Press.*

77 Entrance. Trent designed a cinema entrance which stylishly proclaimed the purpose of the building. Herbert Felton, 1934. Copyright *Architectural Press.*

78 (*opposite*) Interior. This glamorous cinema proscenium reflects Trent's awareness of acoustic necessities; the ceiling curves upwards in a sort of cone shape. Herbert Felton, 1934. Copyright *Architectural Press.*

79 EDMONTON EMPIRE CINEMA, LONDON.

The Edmonton Empire was designed by Cecil Masey and Theodore Komisarjevsky and completed in 1933. Its site was that of the old Edmonton Empire Music Hall which had only been built as recently as 1908, a clear indication of the swift change in allegiance of the general public. Seating 2,500 people, the 'Empire' was remarkable for its 'fog-catching' ventilation system, reminding us that the Victorian 'pea-souper' lasted until after the Clean Air Act of 1956. Komisarjevsky's work on the ultra-modern interior had something in common with the contemporary Dutch De Stijl movement. The organ grills on either side of the proscenium were finished in aluminium. The disappearing organ was considered to be one of the most elaborate in the country when new. Herbert Felton, 1933. Copyright *The Architect and Building News* (B. W. S. Publishing).

80 FORUM CINEMA, KENTISH TOWN, LONDON.
The Kentish Town Forum was designed by J. Stanley Beard and completed in 1934. It could house 2 000 people. The exterior of the cinema was decorated with quasi-Egyptian detailing of black columns set against white faience. A café filled the space over the foyer. Most cinemas were equipped with a café, open to the general public as well as the cinema audience. Herbert Felton, 1935. Copyright *The Architect and Building News* (B. W. S. Publishing).

NEWS CINEMA, VICTORIA STATION, LONDON.
This cinema was designed by A. MacDonald and completed in 1933. The news cinema was a sign of the transformation made by 'talkies' in the field of journalism, and one was installed in most major railway stations in Britain during the 1930s. This News Cinema no longer shows newsreels and is now in poor condition.

81 (*opposite, above*) Exterior. The horizontal lines of this cinema were said to accord more with the lines of the locomotives at the nearby platforms than with the 'antiquated structure' overhead. Herbert Felton, 1933.

82 (*opposite below*) Interior. The barrel roof was a result of having to squeeze the cinema into a confined space in Victoria Station. The acoustics were therefore not ideal. A full house comprised 235 people, many of whom would be commuters. Information on train arrivals and departures was shown on a separate screen to the right of the proscenium. Herbert Felton, 1933. Copyright *The Architect and Building News* (B. W. S. Publishing).

83 (opposite) RITZ CINEMA, SOUTHEND, ESSEX.
The Ritz Cinema was designed by R. Cromie and completed in 1934.
Cromie became the doyen of independent cinema architects and was
responsible for the erection of over fifty cinemas between 1928 and 1940.
He sought to improve the standard of design in cinemas. For the Ritz he
produced an interior which was both modern and elegant. Herbert Felton,
1935. Copyright *The Architect and Building News* (B. W. S. Publishing).

84 GAUMONT PALACE CINEMA, CHELTENHAM, GLOUCESTERSHIRE.
Trent's cinema of 1933 was fitted with one of the accessories which added
so much to the charm of cinema entertainment, the cinema organ. Here
the organist stands beside the illuminated organ, which is a Compton
model. Herbert Felton, 1933.

85 (*overleaf*) ODEON, READING, BERKSHIRE.
The Odeon at Reading was designed by A. P. Starkey and completed in
1937. This was the year of the Coronation of King George VI and Queen
Elizabeth, and every cinema showed the special film which was made of
the historic occasion. It was the first time that the ceremony in
Westminster Abbey was relayed to millions of people in cinemas
throughout the world. This photograph shows the Odeon's foyer
decorated in celebration. Larkin Brothers, 1937.

CLOAKROOM

GRANADA CINEMA, WOOLWICH, LONDON.

The Woolwich Granada, built in 1937, was designed by Cecil Masey and R. H. Uren. The interior, which could seat 2,000 people, was decorated by Theodore Komisarjevsky.

86 The Granada was given a stark functional exterior. This included a tower which was illuminated at night. Herbert Felton, 1937. Copyright *The Architect and Building News* (B. W. S. Publishing).

87 Interior. Komisarjevsky created an exotic pastiche of the Continental Gothic style, in marked contrast to the plain and modern exterior. Herbert Felton, 1937. Copyright *The Architect and Building News* (B. W. S. Publishing).

88 (*opposite*) Projection Room. Herbert Felton, 1937. Copyright *The Architect and Building News* (B. W. S. Publishing).

LONDON FILM PRODUCTIONS STUDIOS, DENHAM, BUCKINGHAMSHIRE.

London Film Productions Studios were built in 1936 for Alexander Korda. They were designed by C. S. and E. M. Joseph with F. Milton Cashmore, in collaboration with Korda's friend Jack Okey, who came over from Paramount's Studios, Hollywood. Denham was the birthplace of many famous British films. Demolished 1980–1.

89 The main frontage, which contained the administration offices and dressing rooms, restaurant and cafeteria. It was 1,000 feet long. Herbert Felton, 1936. Copyright *The Architect and Building News* (B. W. S. Publishing).

90 (*inset, above*) Studios. There were seven studios of vast dimensions, four of which were 250 feet by 120 feet and 45 feet high. The stars reached these studios by glazed and heated covered ways leading from their dressing rooms. The studios were equipped to accommodate all types of lighting and insulated for the best acoustic results available for sound recording. Air extract chambers were at the rear of the studios. Herbert Felton, 1936. Copyright *The Architect and Building News* (B. W. S. Publishing).

91 (*inset, below*) Screening room. The 'rushes' of such great Korda films as *Wuthering Heights* and *Henry VIII* would have been viewed here by their makers. Herbert Felton, 1936. Copyright *The Architect and Building News* (B. W. S. Publishing).

92 BROADCASTING HOUSE, PORTLAND PLACE, LONDON.
The architects of Broadcasting House, completed in 1931, were Val Myers and Watson Hart, but the interior was designed by such architects as Maufe, McGrath, Chermayeff and Wells Coates. An experimental television studio was one of the modernistic studios which they designed. Regular transmissions of television programmes began in 1936 but these were from Alexandra Palace, London. Broadcasting House concentrated on the BBC's radio services, as it continues to do today. Herbert Felton, 1931.

INDEX

References in roman numerals refer to introduction pages. Other references refer to the plates.